MW01273123

Library and Archives Canada Cataloguing in Publication

Knox, V., 1949 - author
I was there / V. Knox.
Poetry.
ISBN 978-0-9937380-8-1 (softcover)
I. Title.
PS8621.N695I93 2016   C813'.6   C2016-907745-4

Editor – Silent K Publishing
Cover design – Veronica Knox & Iryna Spica
Typeset in *Times* and *Poetica* at SpicaBookDesign

First Edition

Printed in Canada

Silent K Publishing:
Victoria, British Columbia
www.veronicaknox.com

e-mail: veronica@veronicaknox.com

I was there

V KNOX

a poem of my travels through time

for

sarah
and
david

The heraldic lion, 'The Marzocco'
– symbol of the Republic of Florence

THE ART OF TIME TRAVEL

– an Epic Poem of an Imagination in Transit –

If meditation is time travel, then I have been there with Leonardo and Sandro and Lisabetta. I brushed against their cloaks of country-rough sackcloth or city-thick velvet trimmed in fur, and run my fingers over the heavy embroidered stuff of their Sunday best. I've worn a wedding gown of stiff pearl-encrusted silk.

I've paced out the length and breadth of the Piazza della Signoria with Il Marzocco (the heraldic lion of Florence) and his wife – the back-to-back lions of yesterday and tomorrow where we skirted the deserted arena, a savannah of sun-baked paving stones, hugging the walls, keeping to the shadows – circling the square, squaring the circle, roaring at its empty coliseum of African dreams, ignoring the pigeons and an escaped wishing-pig. We were careful to sidestep Savonarola's fire-blackened martyr-stone marking the center of vanity, the very heart of art.

I've set aside many a nosegay against the blast of renaissance filth. But then I've also been gifted the scent of flowers blooming free of diesel fumes and pesticides, leaving our bleached versions of fruit and vegetables and pale-scented roses in the dust.

I've shadowed fifteenth-century Florentines unawares, light and casual in my T-shirt and tenderized stone-washed jeans, shuffling through their littered streets in sensible shoes, vaccinated and well-supplied with bottled water.

As a time-traveler, I've explored their natures the way discoverers of the New World embraced the shores of a Utopian mirage. I invited them inside my head, to share one mood, one pair of eyes, and allowed their DNA to mature – to blossom in quiet moments and prosper under my skin.

As their host, I gave them breath and a voice. As an author, I continue to shout their praises in pixels and electrons, and gift them paper and air.

– Veronica Knox 10/4/16

1

I smile between the lines of my travelogue
long before I wake, back-trekking my destinations
for old time's sake.

Where wandering diamonds
fill the night sky with shining questions
in an endless why of juicy suggestions
thrown out by brave voices
once silenced by death and feeble choices,
caught by me, in bold quotation marks
out of the mouths of history.
Earth's heroes reveal their incandescence
as human comets of sentient luminescence
who leave 'a wake' of animated sparks.

3

I wonder...

Are the vapors of events too preposterous to reveal?

or too ridiculously obvious to conceal?

Are the best clones given second chances?

Is it ever too late to expose the times

and shapes of lovers' betrayals

and the weak protesting trysts of love's denials

that edge hand-over-hand at glacier speed

racing the worms?

Sleep, the great movie romance,
has front row beds in a soft theatre
where I play inside a whorl of moonlit chances,
spinning adrift within a vortex of emotion
as a visitor shadow.
I reside fretfully on daydreams and nightmares
hanging on the angel-hair thread of a moonbeam
in an omnipotent blue nebula
that, breathing out of control, sends spiraling memories
to lure clusters of dreamers.
Wonder-driven and ghostly, I fly high, working the
updrafts, wind-taken, buffeted and invisible,
toe-dipping into once-upon-a-time
– an extra in the crowd scenes,
rubbing shoulders with box-office honey,
a fan, schmoozing with the brightest stars.

5

Gravity-soaked, I descend, a happy vampire of truth
heavily drawn to the warmth of living blood,
floating low as a curious passer-by
grasping at random perfumes of the past,
tasting its mystery fruit,
intoxicated from a gallery of true-faces,
to land knee-deep in the poison of a confessional.
Where sins are recorded for old time's sake
in a dark box,
and the stinking lies of verbal blight
are bland contritions in search of sunlight.

6

I freefall slowly through particles of what-was,
to be caught on the spires of an ancient temple.
Now-and-then awake, I drop
from the clear turquoise of an upturned scrying bowl
– one Tuscan sky in early April,
where a copper pearl perched on the fingertip of God
points to the dome-home of a heaven so tranquil
to inspire a seeker suspended above the fumes of rebirth.
Neither there nor here
– a non-believer balancing on a spinning sphere.

New rain falls on ancient streets
and slips down grimy windows of greased paper
yellowed with the forgotten weathers
of anonymous wisdom and dusty rage.
Primeval tricks of archaic light,
– the enchantments cast by eons of eternal fairies,
baptize the chosen mortals, glamour-sprinkled
behind the veils beyond time's portals,
who huddle next to hearth fires
stirring endless pots of soup and salted porridge.
They arise in answer to the church bells
and make their way to shrines,
gasping and praying and bowing their bones
to replicas of reliquaries
encrusted with gemstones made from sugar,
housed under-glass in gingerbread cathedrals
where the finger-bones of saints are dipped in chocolate,
and pawned to the lowest bidder.

Altruistic, and all true-phobic,
and from being none too stoic
and faced with unrelenting, unfolding,
and unalterable fate,
or something untoward I ate.
I trot back to Zeno School with a new backpack
filled with scented magic-markers and remorse.
My back against a tsunami of tainted data,
I highlight my way through faded documents and
crumbling arguments,
with acid yellow trails of pungent ink –
blazing a neon road to Oz –
where the tall wizard of Vinci
forges new games under
the shade of a giant horse.

9

I'm there

when Leonardo conjures a mechanical lion with a tin

heart, to wind-up a childish monarch.

But that royal fool, distracted by new flavors,

betrays art's patriarch, and allows his toy

to fall down the rabbit hole of his-story

— so a priceless lion-king roars

down the slippery slope of mystery.

Far below,

the fallout of an archaeologist's best golden mirage

awaits in a deep cache of cheap thrills

and noble art buried by regret and lead apologies,

polished and sharpened into new mythologies.

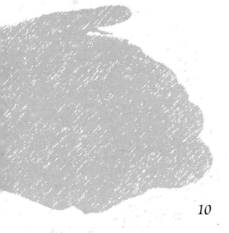

Samothrace's white Victory
– a statuesque goddess once dressed in gaudy bling
for the Hellenistic naval ball,
stands defeated at the top of the stairs, passing the time.
The toppled lighthouse queen's retrograde destiny
hovers, frozen in the space of eternity.
'Nike', a cryogenic lady-in-waiting, held captive
within the stasis of a hermetically sealed museum,
anticipates the technologies of two thousand years
to restore her broken limbs.
An archaeological donor's card of body parts:
to transplant an injured wing
and heal the massive head wounds
of ancient color-blindness
and the shattered windblown draperies of hindsight.

In the shady past, when a greased palm
covered the sun with baksheesh antidotes,
it unleashed the science-friction
of dark and tall back-door anecdotes.
Tell-alls stained with power.
Leonardo was sideswiped by a brief notation
from the brotherhood of platonic accusation
scribbled in the wild by a devious malcontent.
A spasm of soapbox time, archived in amber
that spread dirty rhymes,
and paroxysms of jealousy and lust
unscrupulous convulsions of raw spite
on spare shards of paper,
posted without hesitation or compunction
to the ballot box of harm where truth turns on a dime
whenever a lawyer stirs the pot.

The music of Leonardo's lute,
spills from its jawbone frame,
singing his praises of posthumous fame
and his silent shame.
Lyrics sighing over trembling horsehair strings
and bats wings, and pegs of ivory
and silver tuned to a master's perfect pitch.
And when Leonardo was angry or I heard him laugh,
time gifted me the timbre of his voice that
resonated with masculine grace.

*The 'Bocca della verità' the
mouth of truth – an ancient lie
detector similar to the public
ballot boxes distributedthroughout
Florence where citizens could post
anonymous complaints.*

Only literary rebirth and relentless re-search
could free Lisabetta's caged bird-soul
or credit Leonardo another true iconic gold star.
I separate the persuasive fakes from the sheep
Balancing the genuine attempts
left in the dark by his students and copyists.
Menageries of honest forgeries all in a row
– an elite sisterhood of immaculate deception.
On the face of it, compliments to a beloved master,
but under all, the perpetual Leonardo boy
teased by family, colleagues, and the heartless sons
who had imprisoned him with the look-hooks of love.
Leonardo unplugged, is a warrior teenager
of family dysfunction
and a later self-esteem junkie
burning out his salad years,
both workaholic and erratic,
– a weaver of disenchanted magic
compelled by law to wear the masks of love.
Leonardo, the consummate escape artist
who had lived dangerously – vulnerable
behind the abject busyness of addictive discovery.

LEONARDO – a sixteen-year-old apprentice in the studio of Master Verrocchio.

Once, I interrupted him during a presentation:

"What are you doing here," he said. "Girls aren't allowed."

I told him to get used to it. He smiled at that, and I was hooked.

He was my first teenage crush.

I have stood enchanted beside Leonardo, the alchemist,
and watched an incubus
spring from the flames of sulphur.
And awed by the pious, Leonardo,
dreaming a holy painting onto stretched paper with
rust-colored chalk.
I have sat at his side as he scribbled in code
beside midnight candles.
Watched him lean weary elbows upon
a tallow-dripped table piled with
tattered manuscripts
and the wings of dead birds,
and room temperature ideas left to boil.
Checked the Petrie dishes of
his fresh thoughts,
brain-simmered and
juicy, ready to spawn.

15

I have daydreamed on the riverbanks, where
renaissance stories collide gently
on the mudflats of the Arno
laundered over the rocks of make-believe,
delivered to the ears of a beach.
Tales immortalized by the ink of a passing teacher
who volunteered to reach into the future.
I visited a civic sculpture garden
– a sunlit petting zoo of stone lions
and the rearing white meat of Carara's marble-fleshed
horses, and rubbed a pig's nose for luck in the marketa.
I've seen it turn from bronze to fool's gold
from too many greedy wishes.

I have tarried in the throng of a brutal piazza
guarded by the claws of Marzocco,
choking on the befouled air of its vanity fire
and the gathering stink of martyrdoms and heretics
and executions of vengeance and comeuppance
that dangled from the windows of a violent city hall.
And I turned to observe a young Leonardo in the bustle,
casually sketching the limp body of a traitor

as it swung heavily on political ropes
from a makeshift gallows.
– a common or garden window sill
where we plant flowers
and the fifteenth-century displayed frightening
consequences of involuntary justice.

*c. 1473 – the earliest known landscape by
Leonardo - age 21*

I remember my 'First Supper' with Leonardo.
A table for two, set under a wild moon,
sampling thin-slicings of life
presented on a golden platter.
We passed tidbits back and forth of a personal matter
which involved a second-seating of dainty dishes,
porcelain finger-bowls, and a boat of gravy wishes.
He and I dined on information bytes
– light snacks of vicarious fame
served with a side order of lies
and the high-fat intimate content of newly-spilled beans.
I was determined to make a meal of it
and Lisabetta was hungry for publicity.
Other meals were a dog's breakfast of false information,
but the tastiest was an honest buffet
spread on a table as long as the food chain of history
– an all-you-can-digest feast of surprises

with a third course of just desserts and birthday cakes.
Leonardo and Lisabetta fared alternate repasts
of gluttony and seasonal starvation;
they told me so as we sipped tea and sympathy
in the afternoons.
There were lengthy meals of tasteless rumors and the
lowest calories, but I wanted fast-food ordered to-go.
Stimulants for the road
– my short time-sensitive windows
in a personal tour of deadlines.
It takes ages to read a mystery menu
written in foreign magic.
I wake with portable morsels to digest later
– tragic leftovers carried home in a tinfoil swan.

Daybreaks and sunsets remind me
that Leonardo and I share the same planet.
His rain and mine were equally wet.
We both puddle-splashed barefoot
through mud and water.
My century's snow is as crystal white and chill as his.
Our winds blow hot and cold
in-time to the same rhythms of the moon's pull.
The spectrum of landscape greens and sky-blues
refresh our vision.
Roses and lemons and damp earth deliver the subtleties
of heaven-scent grace.
Our collective need for beauty spans generations.

The pursuits of pleasure and the anguishes of pain rack
our nervous sensibilities to bliss or shreds.
As always, we are slave to the chatter of an incessant
monkey overlord,
prey to our own propaganda of self doubt...
By varying degree, we know the same appetites
of love and fear.
Loneliness and sadness and remorse
remain our diseases of default.
Hate and jealousy rear the same ugly heads.
The grape intoxicates as ever.
Science is where the first crack begins to show;
religion is where it ends in the great divide
of intellect or superstition.

But now, faith in god is unsafe.
Up for clean atheistic grabs...
on the table, biopsied with intellect –
the ultimate social and moral dissection
without prejudice.
The dire consequences of mother church's tortures and
executions are circumvented
with human rights and reasonable protections.
The color spectrum is as constant as a rainbow.
And math, the one eternal truth, is a treasure of sacred
gold underneath creation.
Even now, modern art fights old wolves at new doors.
Artists in hand-to-teeth combat,
up against walls of financial substance
not significantly different from Leonardo's.
Altruistic patrons notwithstanding
A good commission, or man, or woman
is still hard to find.
Technology sets us apart; art unites us,
but our wishes are still governed
by the whims of flying pigs.

*I loved to tease him. I always called this
diagram, 'Leonardo trying to fly'*

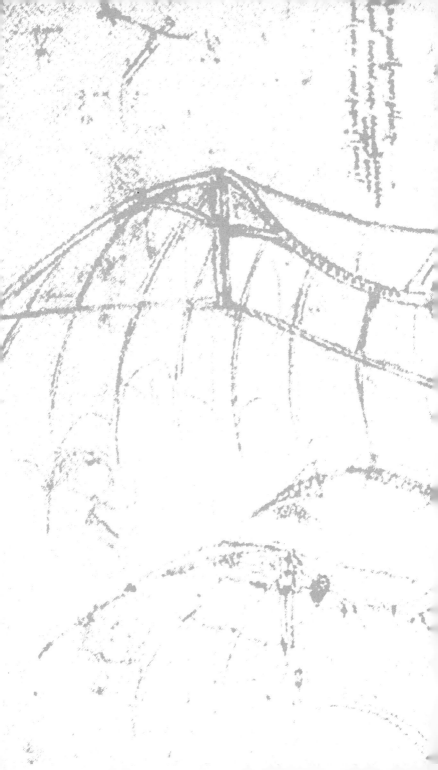

20

I have heard the breath catch in Leonardo's throat
with a fervent wish as he dared to cope,
and seen his knuckles whiten with hope
as his ornithopter approached the edge of the void
heaving itself like an arthritic dragon into the sky
to greet the pale swan-shaped clouds of daybreak that
cling to Mt. Ceceri.

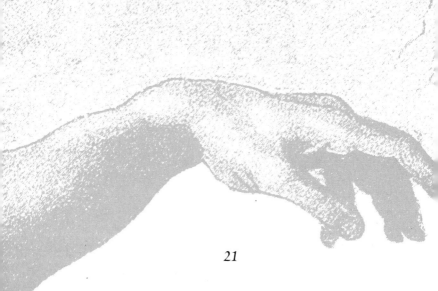

21

Faces have deliberately turned towards me
to reveal the colors of their eyes
and the depth of their need to be remembered
While I stood unobserved and alone
noting the fabric of their cloaks and the profiles of
genteel bones.
I have studied the Sistine masterpiece
before the soot of a thousand desperate candles
turned it sallow from too many prayers.

I breathed in the scents of art and the violet shadows of
the setting sun, leaning against the campanile
soaking up the language of their excitements and
grievances – bereft from loss and disturbances
of abandonment and argument
or delirious from lusting and craving
unsweetened consummated love.

I have stalked the guilty footsteps of the little devil, Salai,
who remembered only the creative truth
as he glided towards depravity.
His boots of calf leather inches below the old paving
stones of yesterday's Via Ghibellina,
feet desperate with evasion
– his fear flying ahead
like a bat from a midnight clock tower
whenever he sensed the authorities closing in.
And many times I ducked into a shallow mauve
doorway to avoid Botticelli, shuffling and old,
his eyes wide with the terrors of religion.

I am a literary sponge,
there to absorb the first rays of light
which filter through the heavy scent of lemons
that wafts down to Firenze from the slopes of Fiesole.
I stroll the inner sanctum of the city's heart,
running my fingers over the polished toes of art
and the coarse cornerstones of the Medici Palace,
and saunter through the wide open doors of the studios
– both Leonardo's and Verrocchio's.
Carefully walking between the great tables
groaning with the weight of sculpture,
mindful to preserve the sacred dust of culture
that settles from the ashes of cold kilns
and the dry summer streets.

I thirst for more,
the way sunlight drinks from a fountain,
travelling in the armchair of my own room
to gather the August olives of Campo Zeppi
and woven green wicker baskets in September
that dry to domestic bliss by November.
And trimmed the wicks of midnight candles
on the frosty feast of Mithras.
I have journeyed far,
and landed fly-on-the-wall obscure,
to watch a mechanical lion slowly inch forward
towards a king...
majestically creaking toward its stately exit.
But I already know a toy species can suffer velveteen
extinction from the shortness of a regal attention span.
So I followed the blasphemous Leonardo,
and the scapegoats of yellow dogs,
and the Templars with their sacrificial women,
down into the chilly catacombs of Rome
where cults and seers divined my future
and, insight be damned, I could at least put them right.

Lisabetta and I fast-forwarded past the girly small-talk.
I spent quality time reading her childhood palms,
calculating her years ahead of lifeline sin.
And listened to a mature Lisabetta wagering on heaven,
who had studied charts of astrological tendencies
to avoid the perils of earthly hell.
She was Giocondo-phobic.
Wary of her second-hand friend yet trusting me.
And after a few visits with animated twin portraits,
I learned how a pair of oil and water women –
double Lisas, side-by-side,
deferred to the master's vision.
Inspiring the same Leonardo to different effect.

As Lisabetta's custodian
I filled a pharaoh's tomb with her yearnings
and downloaded her fallen stars
into a ticking time-capsule.
Her thousand dreams (the macrocosm and the
miniscule) were crushed together –
with wishes and occult confidences
from the illogical to the phenomenal,
having been traced through the houses of the
astrological.
From horizon to horizon, I met the cusps
and the meridians of Lisabetta's successes.
Plumbing her inheritance
of homespun failures and distresses.
Noting each delicate astronomy and hard-pressed
economy – the celestial and the bestial,
I bore witness to her zeniths and eclipses,
and held her hand during her oppositions and trines.

We shared worlds: I gifted Leonardo
the miracles of Polaroid and DVD.
I offered him stereophonic Mozart
on a yellow Walkman
– the same dimensions as the pocket-sized libricini,
the small notebooks kept strung at his waist.
The pure child of him revealed a man delighted
by all manner of futuristic workings –
from the swoosh of a deployed umbrella
to the click of a ballpoint pen.
He bequeathed me his learning-curve
of diagrams and proofs –
a 'Vitruvian' display of sacred proportion.
I saw a human moth pinned by a lepidopterist
– the self-portrait of an alchemist
spread-eagled in a witchy circle.

The art of anthropology arrived like a snake eating its
tail, full-cycle
– the measure of a man's two dimensional ideals
contained in a bursting folio of sketches and in-situ jots,
and a leather diary which contained a blizzard of
prophecies and yearnings in code.
Inside, were lists of Leonardo's debacles of fate
and the lushness of his heart's secret poetry
– memories torn to confetti
tossed in a snowstorm of pixels.
They fluttered from his sky to my earth.

I have accompanied the extent of Lisabetta's fatigue
A renaissance woman, lost in the surrounding ooze
of da Vinci intrigue.
The mirror image of Leonardo's discriminating powers
of observation, silent as the grave's muted conversation
as she shifted her weight in a hard-back chair
while Leonardo laboured
over a single rosy fingernail and a tendril of hair.
Describing a perfect, delicate cuticle while calculating
a degree of ellipse that was never there,
foreshortened, as it was,
in the perspective of creative license.

I have witnessed the citizens of Milan
as they wept over love,
and rejoiced over the deaths of their enemies,
and survived the hungers of red plague
and emotional pestilence.
I recorded a thousand fragments of organic
imagination... history and her-story.
The feminine and masculine dynamic of plain folk,
dazzled and besotted by saints,
but afraid of their own angels.

And while reinventing the dance of Hydrogen
with familiar strangers
I shared time with phantoms in a singularity of hours
hearing echoes of passing juxtapositions
and conversations floating down wine-soaked streets,
drifting aimlessly from palaces and hovels,
and the love-stained sheets of the brothels.
I stalked art that sneaked past the guardian, Janus,
measuring irrefutable miles of provenance,
mapping the truest longitude and latitude
of overgrown land-escapes
and the intimate territories of a portrait's shining
countenance for me to discover
copious copies of copies of copies.

I dined with Leonardo at his Last Supper
of minestrone and bread.
Watched a silver spoon fall from his grasp in slow
motion; heard it clatter upon an oak table
as he reached for a grail of spiced wine.
The air, violet-scented and electric,
mixed with leftover April sunbeams
twisted into an evening maelstrom
when thunder and lightning
approached the Loire Valley
to play silhouette tricks around the walls of Clos de Luce.
Leonardo had received death alone as Cecco slept.
I was the intruder as Lisabetta helped his spirit to the
window where, to his delight... he flew.
The aftermath of the next morning
revealed fallen trees, and unfinished soup,
and the 'Mona Lisa's empty pedestal.
Abandoned art at the end of the rainbow.

It has been my quest to restore the missing credits
and the shattered business of art,
and paste together the pages torn from burned diaries,
and take mental snapshots of lost paintings.
Privy to the casual messages of contrapposto,
I have translated every gesture of the Mona Lisa's hips
and traced the secret language of her lips.
And the obscure nuances of her invisible eyebrows
told me everything I needed to know.
And once, Lisabetta saw me shimmering in a mirage,
leaning over Leonardo's shoulder as he painted her,
and she sent me an impassioned plea:
"write it for him as well as me,"
and I understood she meant Sandro.
So how could I ever forget the radiant thanks she sent me
when I told her that I would, of course I would?

And so, I took my leave
and left her dreaming in a French prison
where she awoke, smiling.

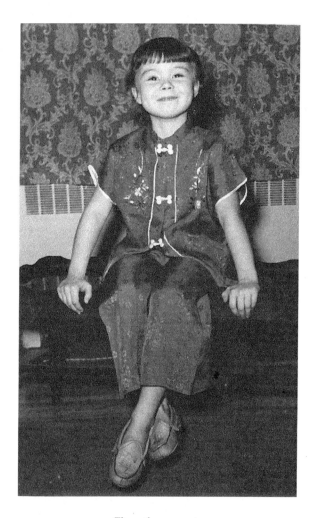

The author – age six

My history

I was delivered by a stork with a twisted sense of humor and a muddled sense of direction. A note that said: *'this is no ordinary kid'* was attached to my ankle. I had been saddled with delusions of future grandeur. I was dropped in an English home where furniture, carpets, curtains and shoes were all beige or brown. Ugh. No wonder I paint pictures on floors and colored furniture. **please see my website*.

But in spite of those dreary bedroom curtains *(in the picture)*, dragged to Canada from the homeland, I was the bee's knees because I had the red silk pajamas prove it. I realize a black & white photograph fails to show this, but look at my expression. Those curtains were brown but the pajamas were cherry red, and I wanted to wear them to school. I wanted a pair of scarlet Mary-Janes like Dorothy from 'The Wizard of Oz'. I expected Canada to be paved with yellow brick roads and shops that sold red shoes.

Alas, I was sent to my first Canadian school decked out in a pair of brown oxford lace-ups, and an outfit of several non-resplendent shades of beige. It took a year to grow from a princess-in-the-bud to a wallflower kid who kept to the shadows lest some dull spark of a classmate blew my cover.

Score one for the droll stork.

Besides, those flower faces in the curtain pattern scared the stuffing out of me. They said terrible things like *"Kid! you're not going to be a swan, so you might as well get used to being ordinary."* They insisted *"the future is grim." "Never trust a stork,"* they said.

But, the key word in their prophecy was 'future'... as in another time and place. And being a perverse child, I chose to interpret 'grim' as an invitation to read more fairy tales.

Children's television, then in its infancy, offered lackluster cartoons and lame puppet shows, but books gave me princes and paupers, and secret gardens, and a rabbit with no time to waste.

I dug my own rabbit hole and made a nest. I was mole in search of the natural home that the stork missed. I was, as the 'Moody Blues' later explained to me in a song-poem, gestating *'the days of future passed'*.

The first time I read Victorian and Edwardian children's books, I knew I could time travel. I followed Peter Pan to the first star on the right, camped out in a Wendy House under a clock with no hands, and experienced an extraordinary butterflying of the senses through the eyes of an extremely stoned caterpillar.

I was in awe of animal characters who wore clothes, and a bear who lived in a house at Pooh Corner. I coveted Alice's blue dress and white pinafore.

Books led me, a budding author intent on listening to the wind in my own willows, down a path to a different curtain. Behind this veil was an imaginary world where anything could happen. I visited fairies at the bottom of the garden and swam with the water babies. I lived in Victorian times, thrilled to be 'seen and not heard'. I was an invisible child with invisible friends and an invisible muse.

Retreating into a writer's cave was the next step. My first writer's cave was an abandoned closet that was more of a long low crawl space with a three-foot door under the eaves of our old house. Equipped with candles and a cardboard box for a table, I wrote and produced the proverbial 'kid's neighborhood newspaper' and sold three copies: to my father, a grandmotherly lady who lived next door, and Mrs. Orchard who lived in a frozen pocket of time, down one of the only country lanes in our cold concrete city.

Looking back, I remember walking my bicycle to the entrance of her tree-lined street where I entered a world as fantastic as any accessible from the back of a wardrobe. After tea and fairy cakes I emerged from her back alley carrying huge pink peonies to take home for my mother. I believed time swallowed the entrance so I never looked back until fifty-years later. Diagon Alley reminded me of that time I almost forgot.

But that's what remembering childhood is… it's time travel. It's when a boy named Max travels across an ocean to a distant land and has several heart-stopping adventures with 'the wild things' but comes home weeks later to find his dinner is still hot.

For me, it's revisiting a past and future that later as an author, I can embellish with the art of what-if. What if a famous painting could talk? And what if, by touching its frame, I find myself in the fifteenth-century? All those paintings with the sad label 'now lost' can tell me what happened. And more importantly, where they are.

Art history is one of my favorite subjects. Time travel allows me to watch paintings being created and hover as a 'fly on the wall' to witness the human lives unfolding beneath me. And hear directly from the painting's mouth, about the days when they were mislaid or stolen or destroyed. So naturally, I invent time-travelers who can go back to retrieve them and perchance fall in love and stay there.

Words reach for a peak experience. Words in a book strive to deliver more than regular speech but less than formal poetry. But then I stumbled into T.S. Eliot's 'The Love Song of J. Alfred Prufrock.' His wonderful gestalt of organized word-salad observed from afar, hooked me.

Poetry from the heart is never showing off. Quite the contrary... it's an ushering in.

'I WAS THERE' is my personal invitation to meet me by the wishing pig in the fifteenth-century market of Florence and share a futuristic espresso. To time travel inside my mind that records what others may not but wish they could.

My poem wasn't crafted. It came as it came. Fast, fluid, and bright. Which proves to me that poetry is the purest literary form where muse and writer are inseparable.

V KNOX

MORE V. KNOX TIME-TRAVEL NOVELS

middle-grade, Y/A, and art historical literary fiction time-slip mysteries

'SECOND LISA' – *a fanciful trilogy of Leonardo da Vinci's historical half-sister, Lisabetta Buti.*

The embittered spirit of the 'Mona Lisa,' trapped inside her portrait, escapes from the Louvre and causes havoc in an autistic boy's world view in order to be recognized for her true identity

book one – Lisabetta's childhood
book two – the studio years
book three – middle age and legacy

'ADORATION – loving Botticelli' – *a paranormal romance.* A retired art history professor, haunted for years by a self-portrait of the artist Sandro Botticelli, is lured into one of his masterpieces to consummate their romantic longings for each other, five-hundred-years in the past.

THE PEARL SERIES: – science-fiction time travel with a strong female protagonist, asks *will it take two lives to make one woman?*

'THE INDIGO PEARL' *book one of two.* After being trapped in an extended near-death experience, Delphi Sharpe, a female savant with the telepathic ability to converse with paintings, has her brain implanted into the circuits of Cherry White – a time-traveler android programmed to retrieve missing masterpieces in the distant past. But the donor and the recipient are at odds over sharing a soul and reclaiming the heart of a teenage boy in a five-hundred-year-old portrait who eclipses their singular goal of destroying the institution that exploited them.

'PEARL BY PEARL' *book two of two.* The story concludes in the continuing afterlife, past-life, and future life of two women. With the same memories rivalling for the ghostly lover they now share, two female 'art-whisperers' must struggle against their conflicting goals to mine the distant past for sentient paintings willing to divulge the secrets of their shared lost identity.

THE BEDE SERIES: *late middle-grade (age 11 to 14) / young adult (age 15 to 19)*

'TWINTER – the first portal'– a late middle-grade time-slip mystery *book one of 'The*

Bede Series' Bede Hall, an abandoned stately home near Hadrian's Wall, is desperate. It must rally its dispersed family before it's sold to developers. Its new residents, a pair of thirteen tear-old twins, must rescue a girl lost in time whose apparition has haunted the estate for generations. But rescue only opens a time portal that reveals terrible secrets.

BEDE titles in progress:

'TIME FALLS LIKE SNOW'– a Y/A timeslip adventure *book two of 'The Bede Series'* Bede Hall, a sentient building with a timely past, harbors further disturbing phenomenon. The secrets of Bede Hall continue with the sixteen-year-old twins working in league with a team of ghosts and 'twice-borns' who have been monitoring the time portal's secrets for hundreds of years. It falls to Bede Hall's time corridors, the Great Sphinx of Egypt, the rules of twindom, the magic power of nine, and a team of teenagers with several otherworldly allies to save earth from an alien curse. The 'Twinters' have six years to try in a landscape where history is positively ancestral.

'TOMORROW NEVER COMES'

'TEMPTING FATE'

'THINGS TAKE TIME'

'TIMING IS EVERYTHING'

ADDITIONAL HISTORICAL TIME-SLIP
MYSTERIES:

'THE UNTHINKABLE SHOES'– *a surreal
story inspired by a museum exhibit of child's
shoes from the Titanic* – An extraordinary love
story of reincarnation and sacrifice about a boy
who loses his shoes between heaven and the deep
blue sea. When death separates two children on
the Titanic who were destined to marry, the ghost
of the boy chooses to remain earthbound as the
surviving girl's invisible childhood companion in
order to reach heaven. Finding a pair of lost shoes
is their one chance to stay together.

'WOO WOO – the posthumous love story of Miss
Emily Carr' – *a fictional biography that begins
where Emily Carr's true memoirs end.* The Artist
Emily Carr, an eccentric iconic spinster, comes
to her senses sixty-seven years after her death
and calls down the energy of her animal totem,
Woo the monkey, to rekindle the love of a rejected
suitor – a fanciful tale inspired by Emily Carr's
memoirs.

*an homage to the iconic artist of the author's
hometown, Victoria, on Vancouver Island*

www.veronicaknox.com

Walking their talk

Sometimes, to understand history, you must put yourself in another person's shoes.

Walk with me. Pretend for a moment that you are a master painter. You live in fifteenth-century Florence. It takes you over a year to complete a masterpiece. One particular portrait is more important than all the others. This one you tweak when the mood strikes. It will never be finished when you can add another layer of varnish to make it sing. It's not only a new treatise on portraiture, it's the likeness of your beloved sister. A sister who died not long after she posed with her hands just so, and her eyes meeting yours in a familiar return of affection.

She inspired you to greater heights, and so the likeness is not only a perfect representation of her true appearance but also her inner beauty. Her expression mirrors her sense of playfulness as much as the sadness she felt when she lost her only child. You've painted her life by capturing her very soul on a panel of poplar wood. And in your grief you turn to it. You speak to it the same way a photograph in a locket becomes greater than a treasure – a companion with whom you can share your triumphs. A compassionate face that looks back at you and smiles in celebration or empathy.

When you travel, the painting goes with you. When you set up a new home, it's there displayed where you can see it. It's not a formal shrine. It's more like setting a place at the table for a loved one who is never coming home, begun as a gesture to ease your pain. And before too long it IS your sister. She IS home. You speak with her as if she were in the room, and others hear you.

But you are an eccentric man and revered for your unique abilities. What you do is humored and documented: *'Leonardo carried one portrait with him everywhere and would not be parted from it'*. You are Leonardo da Vinci. The portrait becomes celebrated and known the world over as 'The Mona Lisa'- the iconic image of your sister, Lisabetta – the woman known as your half-sister Lisabetta Buti. But you know a secret. She is the second lovechild of your mother and Piero da Vinci. Your relationship is as close as twins born six years apart. You taught your kid sister how to paint. She taught you how to survive.

Later, your painting is the most famous face in the world but Lisabetta's identity is gone. Your sister's name is lost because you painted another Lisa, and somehow the two women have been mistakenly interchanged. The silk merchant's wife's portrait was lost long ago. And now your sister survives as an exquisite portrait, a single line in a forgotten census, and the legend of an old man who carried a portrait to his deathbed... and still, when you leave your body, you will not be parted from her.

Time passes in the otherworld. You can hear Lisa calling. She's trapped by the very art that created her. You search the world over for five-hundred-years. She searches for you too... and at last you meet again through a chance encounter with an autistic boy visiting a museum. A boy who recognizes truths hidden in the open. He feels the magic of a special day – the five-hundredth anniversary of Lisabetta's death. But it's not by chance. Love such as yours never is.

And now 'The Mona Lisa' smiles more radiantly as her new journey begins.

*Down there are familiar streets. Doors that protected people
I knew as family: Leonardo, Sandro, Lisabetta, and the other
anonymous women who worked with their menfolk in the great
art studios – the bottegas of the masters who produced the finest
paintings and sculptures, and the Stinche where Leonardo, a
vulnerable target for jealousy and false accusations of lust, was
cruelly imprisoned for daring to be too talented and too out in
the open.*

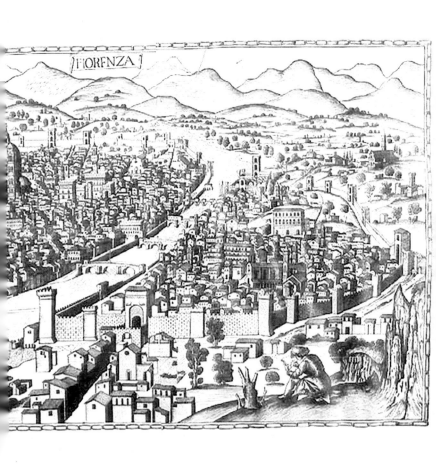